CLIENT-CONSCIOUS PROSPECTING™
How To Overcome Call Reluctance
and Reach Your Full Sales Potential!

by
Steve McCann

CLIENT-CONSCIOUS PROSPECTING ™

How to Overcome Call Reluctance and Reach Your Full Sales Potential!

By Steve McCann

© 2008 Steve McCann Productions~ www.SteveMcCannPro.com

Published by Ashton Square Publishing

Printed in the United States of America

Library of Congress Cataloging-in-Publication Data
2008904492

McCann, Steve

Client-Conscious Prospecting/ Steve McCann

Includes appendixes

ISBN: 978-0-9800359-0-2

1. sales 2. self-help: performance 3. Client-Conscious Prospecting (Title)

For more information about ordering additional copies of this book at special quantity discounts, please visit www.MakingChangeSimple.com

Endorsements for
Client-Conscious Prospecting™

"An entertaining read! Steve understands the difference between selling yourself and serving others; and why those who service sell so much more."

Dan McDade

Author of *The Truth About Leads*

President of PointClear, the Prospect Development Company

"This book is refreshing in that it is truly putting the spotlight on the prospect's needs – not just paying lip service. When a highly conscious salesperson genuinely shifts their focus, they alleviate their fear of prospecting."

Connie Kadansky,

CEO of Exceptional Sales Performance

"Connect with the principles in this book and you'll connect with your most confident self!"

Richard Fenton, Co-author *Go for No!*

"Steve makes selling automatic and simple."

Eric Papp

Generation Y Results-Based Consulting, LLC

Developing and Retaining Gen Y employees/customers

"An easy read. A fast read. A wonderful read. An exciting read. An inspiring read. 'Client-Conscious Prospecting' presents a new mind-set for the selling professional that will take your sales success to levels you've only imagined!"

David Glickman

Author of *Punchline Your Bottom Line: 76 Ways To Get Any Business Audience Laughing*

"*Client Conscious Prospecting*™ serves as a compass for those who wish to stay on track in work and in life. It is a guide for thinking, acting, and believing that no professional, who also has a life, or needs one, should be without!"

Monica Wofford

Author of *Contagious Leadership* and CEO of Contagious Conferences

DEDICATION

This book is dedicated to my wife Diana.

My proof that God answers prayers.

TABLE OF CONTENTS

ACKNOWLEDGEMENTS

This book would not be possible without the help and support of a lot of people. I'll do my best to thank everyone I can but knowing full well that I won't cover all of the fine people (both personally and professionally) who inspired me in some way by their philosophy of life. A special thanks to:

- My wife Diana whose love, strength, and professional skills made this book a reality.
- Our boys Cade and Shane who teach me life skills on a daily basis.
- Mom and Dad, thanks for caring so much throughout the years.
- My brothers, Mike and Dan, who have been confidants and guides along the journey of life.
- Countless family, friends, and colleagues who provided excellent feedback concerning the material held within this book.
- All my friends at the National Speakers Association who encouraged me to write this book.
- My editor and jacket design pro, Kris Maveus-Evenson and her staff at Progressive Ideas Inc. whose professional expertise will be forever appreciated.

Client-Conscious Prospecting™

Introduction

Introduction

The primary responsibility of sales professionals is to prospect for new business. After all, the businesses don't grow if new customers aren't found!

But here's the irony: The greatest challenge faced by sales people is that the very thing we are employed to do and is necessary for the survival of the company we work for is the thing we dread the most - prospecting.

Prospecting is work and, for most of us, a very challenging job filled day in and day out with various forms of rejection. The avoidance of prospecting stems from our own inner desire to protect ourselves from feeling pain - the pain of rejection.

In my nearly two decades as a sales professional and trainer, it has been both my personal experience and observation that sales people with a greater tolerance to rejection make more sales, more money, and enjoy a more relaxed emotional life than the average sales professional.

I am a firm believer that the driving forces which propel athletes to super-athletes are the same forces which also elevate the performance levels of sales professionals. The ability to overcome rejection stems out of how a person views rejection - their mental approach so to speak.

Humans have a basic instinctive need to feel safe. Not one of us wants to feel rejected, no matter how "tough" we may think we are! So we gravitate toward things that will maintain, and even protect, our feelings of safety. Prospecting procrastination actually fulfills our need for this security because if we don't act, we won't risk rejection. After all, if you don't step into the flames, no one gets burned!

In the world of psychology it is widely known that an individual's view of rejection is a core emotion based on past abandonment's, inadequacies, and rejection experiences. Getting to the heart of the complicated subject of rejection involves delving into and altering an individual's past programming - complicated stuff! None of that will be covered here.

In a simpler way, this book serves to provide a practical path for sustaining uncommon activity levels and improving sales production regardless of past programming, personality types, or cognitive I.Q.s. It delivers a simplified mental approach that can virtually eliminate the experience of rejection. If an individual's current perception of rejection no longer exists, then neither does the anxiety he or she attached to it from past programming.

Take a moment to ponder with me....

If rejection could be eliminated, how many new sales could you make on a weekly basis? Can you imagine the phenomenal sales potential that would exist?

Now, let's take it a step further. If the fear of rejection was impossible to feel, what new market segments could be tapped by overcoming the fear-based thoughts about prospecting?

Wow! The idea of how big the sales opportunities would be suddenly is breath-taking, eh?

To be at ease when selling is just one of the many benefits of Client-Conscious Prospecting™. Helping you to be confident, relaxed, and eliminate your fear of rejection is the purpose of this book. I want to challenge you to change your mental approach and rid yourself, once and for all, of the proverbial elephant in the room and monkey on your back!

Are you ready to reach your full potential?

Great!

Then let's get started.

Client-Conscious Prospecting™

Chapter 1

Make the Shift

> The shift occurs the minute we stop making sales about our needs, and place the focus on the best interests of the customer.

Chapter 1

MAKE THE SHIFT

Early in my selling career I sold telecommunication services to businesses door to door. My selling day was all about me: how much business could I generate, how many cold calls could I make in one day, how could I achieve top sales awards, etc. No matter the "how" or the "what" in my sales day, I made the message (and outcomes) all about me.

Like many sales organizations, my company steadfastly believed that a "no" was simply a veiled request for more information. We were trained in rejection blocking by being well-versed in overcoming the five most common objections: "I'm not interested," "We're not in the market," "The price is too high," etc. As part of the corporate sales philosophy, all sales professionals were told to remain at the prospect's office until we had received a grand total of five "no's."

It became an "us" versus "them" scenario. We would arm ourselves with our well-versed objection blockers, thundering in with our cavalry of information, and surely we would win the sale. Sales was war, and an occasional casualty - high sales representative turn-over, declining customer retention, poor morale, etc. - was to be expected.

One day I eagerly prospected to 52 offices door to door. I started in the garment district in South Miami, moved up the 826 expressway to the warehouse district in West Miami, and finished my day in West Fort Lauderdale. I spoke to many people, confident that with enough contacts, I would eventually make a sale. But despite my eager efforts, I made zero sales that day.

At the end of the day, I called in to speak to my sales manager, hoping for a little pep talk. I still can recall the feeling of utter defeat.

I reported, "I received no's from 52 people today." What I didn't say was that with each "no," a small part of my confidence was chipped away. I had to admit that I was taking each "no" personally; making each one I received about me. By the end of the day, it was no wonder that my spirit was broken and my ego wounded.

After speaking with my sales manager, I was convinced that daily rejection was just part of the business of selling. I'd just need to pull myself up by my bootstraps, toughen up, and charge forward. After all, my sales manager assured me, sales was just a numbers game. And so, the next day, I mustered up my courage and went back out into the sales "war zone" and tried once more to win at the game of sales. I dreaded the process of getting back out there, especially after high rejection days.

What I didn't realize was that the problem really wasn't in my sales ability. The trouble lay in the flawed sales formula, which I was trying to use to generate business. I was focusing my sales efforts toward what was best for me - how things affected me, my needs, my goals. No matter how you looked at it, I made selling about me.

At the time, my emotions were attached to my outcomes in my prospecting day. If I was performing well (e.g. I was generating sales), I felt accepted and loved my job. But when I wasn't closing sales or was rejected, I felt depressed and hated every second I was selling. All of my feelings of success hinged on the reactions from others. A career that is based upon the reaction of others makes for a mighty uncomfortable job and leads quickly to burn-out.

It's no wonder I played the game of prospecting procrastination for so long. I didn't want to feel rejection and I didn't have to as long as I didn't make a call.

Brian Tracy, author of *Psychology of Selling* says that the average salesperson doesn't make a sales call until 11 a.m. Based on my own experiences in sales, I doubt that most salespeople start the day with plans to avoid calls for nearly half a workday. However, the reality is that when reluctance kicks in, half the day has gone by and minimal prospecting has occurred! After all, it is easy to avoid the pain of rejection if we simply never put ourselves in that position, right?

When my seven year old son has a nightmare, he finds what he knows is secure - my wife and me. We represent a feeling of safety for him. Humans instinctively have a need to feel safe – no matter what our age! And, oddly enough, this same need to feel secure is also the same need which drives procrastination.

Call reluctance is driven by fears. Fears such as the fear of rejection (we don't want to be rejected), fear of embarrassment (looking bad), fear of failure (what if I fail?), or fear of success (what if I do succeed) are all relevant in both life and in sales. Our response to those fears is to protect our security (or our comfort zone) by finding unproductive things to do.

We engage in low payoff actions like over-preparing (avoidance) or negative projection (predicting how we think the sales call will likely develop). No matter how you look at it, fear prevents us from prospecting. We don't want to feel vulnerable, and we don't want to step outside of our comfort zone.

The truth is, however, that if we fear prospecting we are being controlled by our own self-consciousness. If the prospect says no, it is easy to feel, even slightly, that the rejection is against us personally. We are, in essence, limiting our potential by the misuse of instinct. It's easy to understand, then, why sales prospecting is one of the most dreaded sales activities. No one wants to feel rejected!

Prospecting reluctance fulfills our need for security, but it is a low payoff behavior. By our inaction, no contacts are made, productive time is wasted, and we tend to feel bad about our inability to generate new business. These low payoff activities ultimately lower or reinforce a poor sales self-image. It becomes a vicious cycle – thoughts that you'll fail to close the deal, avoidance of painful situations, guilt about avoiding prospecting all lead back to more negative thoughts, attitudes, and ultimately, behaviors. If the fear of prospecting is present in our activities, it will never fail to sabotage us at the exact moment when our action is needed most.

Thankfully, however, procrastination can be cured. It is possible our desire for security be fulfilled in such a way that provides a high payoff in both income and personal fulfillment. However, making the transition requires a conscious shift in the way we think. The shift occurs the minute we stop making sales about our needs and place the focus on the best interests of the customer. This approach gets plenty of lip-service and could be considered "common-sense." Yet common sense is not always common practice.

The old Christmas movie *Miracle on 34th Street* features just this principle. In the movie, Kris Kringle as the resident Santa Claus for Macy's department store recognizes that Macy's doesn't carry a particular toy desired by a child. He recommends visiting Macy's greatest competitor, who happens to have the toy in stock.

In disbelief, the Macy's executives watch in horror anticipating the lost sales they will experience by referring a customer to their biggest rival. Ironically, however, this simple act of placing the needs of the customer first catapults Macy's to the top retailer. Customers love the new philosophy, and it isn't long before word-of-mouth has generated so much business for Macy's that they can hardly keep up with the sales!

While *Miracle on 34th Street* is a fictionalized story, it demonstrates that it is impossible to fear a customer when your objective is to help them. When their needs and your willingness to help merge, it creates a winning scenario - for everyone.

By simply pointing our thoughts, feelings, and actions away from our own selfish interests and to the best interests of our customers, our fear is virtually eliminated.

It's important to note that not everyone will want our help and when we offer our help - it just might not be the right time. However, what is important is that by putting the needs of the customer first, you have more opportunities to uncover sales possibilities - you may find out about problems you didn't know existed (and require a bigger solution), you may be referred to another account that can use your help, and so forth.

. . .

In early 2001, I was contracted to provide training to a group of attorneys employed by the U.S. Government's executive branch. I was brought in by a government director who was the supervisor of the group. She had been appointed by President Clinton years before and was retained by the Bush administration in the same capacity.

The group consisted of twenty-two government research and litigation attorneys who had the responsibility of reviewing every lawsuit filed by a government employee in the United States.

I met with the director on a Thursday morning just before the presentation. There were a lot of issues in the department and I was brought in to help address some of them through a full-day motivational training covering, among other things, the psychology of optimism.

I was prepared for the presentation yet felt an underlying anxiety. Fear gripped me when I began projecting how I would be received by this group of powerful people. As I started, the mood was silent and a bit stoic. Undisturbed by the absence of any vocal or facial feedback, I continued with my role as seminar leader hoping that the mood would lighten soon.

Thirty minutes into the scripted presentation, I still was not invoking any kind of verbal or non-verbal communication from this group. My right index finger kept pulling the collar of my shirt, as if I were performing a Rodney Dangerfield skit. I was intimidated and full of fear.

A few minutes before the mid-morning break.....it happened.

I felt this inner voice telling me to stop. In mid-sentence, I became silent. I closed the folder of notes that I had been working from, put them in my briefcase, and shut the overhead projector off. I walked around to the front of the small desk on which my notes previously resided and leaned against the desk. I kept quiet, acknowledged my fear, and felt every painful second of it.

I remember the feeling of "unplugging" from my responsibilities in that moment and becoming totally aware of the fear I was feeling. I recall sensing a deep tension, probably more of a surprised anger come over the room... yet I didn't feel a part of it. I was emotionally detached from the experience even though I was right in the heart of the room.

After leaning on the desk for what was probably no more than a minute I said to my audience, "We are done with that!" gesturing to my packed up notes and slides sitting tightly in my briefcase.

"I'm here for you today. I don't work here, and I'm more than moderately certain that I never will. I'm also not emotionally involved. I want to help. All I ask is that we remain solution-oriented in our input. Having said that, what can you and management do to help each and every one of you to get what YOU want?"

For a moment, the room was so quiet you could have heard a pin drop. I knew I had the attention of everyone in the room. All of a sudden, a room full of emotionless faces began to show some emotion and bodies began to squirm. Eyes opened, hands raised. There was suddenly a flurry of involvement that followed.

Except for a short lunch-break, for the better part of the next five hours we did what people do who genuinely want to help each other. We listened, encouraged each other to be heard, and found a solution that worked for everyone.

During this whole brainstorming and validation session, it never became a dump on management, the President, or the present administration. Rather, with such pragmatic minds in the room, it became a problem-solving forum. What had started out as a gloomy, stoic program turned out to be a prosperous day on both sides. I was invited back to Washington D.C. several times after that to conduct the same workshop with other branches of government experiencing similar issues.

I learned a valuable lesson that day. My inner, self- motivated fears caused me to worry about how the audience would receive or react to me. But I was not there to serve my needs, I was there to serve the needs of my client. When the focus became about them, everything changed - and for the better. I had been hired to help them. The minute I stepped into the role of "helper," my natural abilities took over and the audience was much more receptive. I experienced that "confident self" that exists in all of us. There was no more fear in any way.

When we are focused on the prospects interests and needs, then we are not thinking of ourselves. With this "full engagement" on helping them, we are working from that best place within us; that place that wants to help them without any expectation of direct benefit. This is accessing our most confident self which possesses the ability to prospect anyone, anytime, anywhere in any market segment... that's power! It's also Client-Conscious Prospecting™.

Tips to Help Your Shift

Making the shift to embrace prospecting rather than fear it involves a few simple steps. Make the following a part of your everyday activities and you'll have more business than you ever thought possible.

• Create Your List of 10 .

Pick 10 prospects every week and seek to help them in some way even if it won't directly lead to a sale. Actually, make it a point to put "furthering their interests" as the paramount task for yourself. If helping them is not in the scope of your job responsibility, don't let that be an obstacle. Become a problem-solver, a trusted advisor, or whatever can help them to further their interests. They can be people in your networking circles, past customers, or direct prospects for your products. By simply focusing on helping 10 people per week without fail, you are putting this shift into play. You can create a never-ending stream of new business for yourself.

• Think of Others First.

Remember, the shift occurs the minute you stop making prospecting and sales about your needs.

Therefore, think of the person you're about to prospect. What does he or she really need in terms of what you can offer? Lead with that one thing, be open to learning more about their needs, and you'll find more success. (Don't forget, creating clear, compelling value based on their needs is a high payoff technique. More on positioning value, later in this book).

• Timing Counts.

Always remember two key points: 1) Not everyone will want your help, and 2) When you offer your help it just might not be the right time for the other person. Therefore, you can't take any rejection personally. Again, it's not about you... it's about the other person and what's going on in his or her life or business at that particular time.

The bottom line is that when you are focused on your prospects' interests and needs, you are not thinking of yourself. If you're not thinking of yourself, you cannot be in fear.

Client-Conscious Prospecting™

Chapter 2
Think, Feel and Act
Right Toward Others

Enlightened Self-Interest: *persons who act to further the interests of others ultimately serve their own self-interest.*	Chapter 2 **THINK, FEEL, AND ACT** **RIGHT TOWARD OTHERS**

A young Abraham Lincoln had just left the tailor donning a new suit, a small reward he promised himself once his law practice had begun to prosper. The tailor was surprised to hear from Mr. Lincoln that this was the first new suit he had ever worn. Mr. Lincoln's upbringing was full of poverty characterized by hand-me down clothes. Even in law school his clothing was sewn together from used garments. The proud Mr. Lincoln, Esq. thanked the tailor for his fine work and stepped into the stagecoach with a few of his key staffers. As the horses proceeded toward the next destination, the inside of the coach was filled with strategy and planning for an upcoming legal case.

The coach came to an abrupt stop causing the bunch inside to pile into one another. At that point one of the staffers questioned the driver as to the cause of the sudden standstill. It seemed the recent rains had formed a trench in the middle of the road which was filled with mud. A wild pig was stuck and unable to get itself out. Gasping and squealing with fright, the pig searched for escape.

Overhearing the conversation, Mr. Lincoln peered out to see the exhausted pig struggling for life. After surveying the situation, the driver saw a stable surface to the left which would provide a safe detour around the trench. As he commanded the horses to move left, Mr. Lincoln yelled out to him, "Halt!"

Then Mr. Lincoln took off his jacket and hat as he proceeded to exit the stagecoach, much to the dismay of everyone on board. Even the horses watched in amazement while a well-dressed Mr. Lincoln stepped into the trench and pulled the pig out with every bit of strength he could muster. The pig scurried into the woods rejoicing with squeals.

> By being aware of and servicing the needs of others, we are indirectly reaching our own goals by making our selfishness work 'for' us.

Looking back at his audience, Mr. Lincoln saw only dumbfounded looks staring back at him - man and animal included. With mud covering more than half his body, Mr. Lincoln stepped out of the trench and wiped as much mud off of his body as he could with his hands.

As Lincoln climbed back into the coach, his staffers battled to be the first to ask the question, "Mr. Lincoln, why would you do such an unselfish thing... for a pig?"

Abraham's answer was calm and convicted, "Sir, I didn't do that for the pig, I did it for myself."

. . .

Whether we want to admit it or not, humans are selfish in nature. From the moment we are born, our world revolves around our needs. As newborn babies, humans are programmed to recognize pain and pleasure, which is why most newborns spend a great deal of their awake time crying. They need food, they need a diaper changed, they are too hot or too cold, or they simply want to feel the comfort of a parent loving them.

No matter how you look at it, humans are motivated by pleasure, or desire for things which ultimately result in feelings of happiness. The problem with "human nature" is that we are programmed to act from a place of selfishness because we want to feel good and we want to avoid pain. Whether it is the food we eat, the places we go, the people we talk to, etc., most of us make choices designed to protect us from feeling pain.

The difference which sets apart top performers - be it in sports or in life - is the mentality which motivates their actions.

Wikepedia defines **enlightened self-interest** as:

"A philosophy in ethics which states that persons who act to further the interests of others ultimately serve their own self-interest. It has often been simply expressed by the belief that an individual will 'do well by doing good.' This is in contrast to greed or the concept of 'unenlightened self-interest.' "

(SOURCE: http://en.wikipedia.org/wiki/Enlightened_self-interest, March 2008)

Imagine for a moment the value of self-enlightened, self-interest. It can be useful not only for our sales careers, but in the ease and positive influence we have with the people we encounter on a daily basis. When we think and act for the good of others, as our dominant thought, the more we will attract the things we desire and cherish. In short, our interests will be served, by servicing first the needs of others. By being aware of and servicing the needs of others, we are indirectly reaching our own goals by making our selfishness work "for" us.

Hindu and Buddhist religions refer to this phenomenon as "karma." We may know this by the popular adage, "What goes around comes around."

The good we demonstrate toward others, ultimately will come back to us.

. . .

A few years ago, I was conducting a seminar in Kentucky to a group of salespeople. At the lunch break, I dined at the hotel restaurant with two women who were attendees of the seminar. In the course of the meal these two women, who had never met before, discovered that they had been married to the same man! One woman was currently married to the man, and the other had been divorced from him years earlier.

Every once in a while I would like to be a fly on the wall to be able to listen to a really juicy conversation. On this day I would have been overjoyed to be a fly on the wall, but in Tahiti or Tacoma or anywhere else but in that restaurant. Awkward is a mild description of those first few moments, for all of us! But, a great lesson in right-thinking was yet to come.

The first wife spoke in complimentary terms about the man to the second wife. I listened intently as these two women exchanged stories of their lives and learned that this man had shared nothing but positive stories about each of them with the other.

It seems to me that he represented the first wife as a good person whom he had good thoughts for when he spoke of her to his present wife. She, of course, was doing the same right there at the table.

As a devoted people watcher and a student of human behavior, I believe I can pick up when someone is insincere or being artificially polite. But this was simply not the case. These women were genuinely reveling in the chance meeting.

In the afternoon session, these two ladies sat in the front row next to each other. When we broke into teams for training exercises, I observed as these women selected each other as partners.

What a privilege it was to witness two (three, if you count the right-thinking husband) mature human beings living out the principle of right thought, feeling, and action!

During my lunch encounter with these women, I learned that the first wife was so successful in her sales career that she worked only eight months of the year and the other four months she did missionary work abroad in poverty-stricken countries.

The present wife also was successful in selling and shared how she and her husband are animal lovers with acres of land filled with exotic animals. She openly discussed how they loved to travel abroad as much as they could to experience new lands and discover new creatures native to these lands.

I don't believe it was accidental that both of these women had financial success or that they were living their bliss. Their dominant thoughts attracted harmonious people into their life. They attracted wealth and what didn't go unnoticed by me is that they lived a very deliberate life. By that I mean that they were doing (e.g. volunteerism in third world countries, traveling abroad, caring for animals) exactly what they wanted, they were living the lifestyle of their own choosing. How many people do you know who could say this about their lives?

> There are no secret thoughts which is why judgment is such a double-edged sword.

What you think of another sets a standard in your subconscious mind, which then applies it to you. There are no secret thoughts, which is why judgment is such a double edged sword. We can never escape a single thought we have, be it about ourselves or about others! If we play slave to negative emotions, it is of our own doing.

The Law of Attraction says that we attract the people and circumstances into our lives through our dominant thoughts and feelings. So by this attraction law, if our dominant thoughts are on how can I maximize my sales and how can I get business from this customer, then we are operating from dominant thoughts of greed. With this self-conscious attitude, selling becomes a grind. It's because our dominant thoughts are selfish. We will actually attract resistance from others, bringing out the selfishness in them. Think back to times when you've encountered pushy salespeople who were clearly out for themselves. Did you want to buy from them? Did you want to go along and cooperate with them?

Selling is about building trust with the client so they feel comfortable to open up about their needs, so you can help them. Self-conscious salespeople have a hard time building that trust and, therefore, have up and down months filled with rejection and resistance.

If we place our dominant thoughts on furthering the interests of those we serve without any expectation of direct benefit, then it's a double-win. This is because we are projecting the best part of ourselves. The prospect can tell when someone shows genuine concern in helping them and has their best interests at heart. So, by the Law of Attraction, we will attract and bring forth that place in them that is cooperative and wants to help us. This Client-Conscious approach meets with little resistance and simplifies the selling process.

THINK, FEEL AND ACT RIGHT TOWARD

OTHERS

- When we think, feel, and act for the good of others as our dominant thought, the more we will attract the things we desire and cherish. In short, our interests will be served by servicing first the needs of others.

- Selling is about building trust with the client so they feel comfortable to open up about their needs so you can help them. This Client-Conscious approach meets with little resistance and simplifies the selling process.

Client-Conscious
Prospecting™

Chapter 3
Sell the Value that You
Would Buy

Chapter 3

SELL THE VALUE

THAT YOU WOULD BUY

> Preparation is
> where success
> is truly found.

Years ago I lived in a Hollywood Beach apartment. Located just below my apartment on the second floor lived Chuck Munroe - a thirty- something salesman from Biloxi, Mississippi. He had an engaging personality and I liked being around him.

Each day I would walk down to my car to go to work, and Chuck would be on his balcony dressed for work, casually drinking his coffee. I knew Chuck was in sales, but for six months, I never knew what it was that he sold. It just never came up in the course of any conversation.

One morning I decided to ask Chuck, mainly out of curiosity, what it was that he sold.

His response was so enjoyable that I missed my morning sales meeting knowing that I was getting a lesson in selling that was far more valuable than the standard sales meetings which occurred in my company.

Chuck was a salesman for commercial tissue and towel products. His thick Mississippi accent saying the term "toilet tissue and towel" was unforgettable. It wasn't just what he said; it was the way in which he said the words. The enthusiasm and pride was equivalent to that of a proud parent who just watched his child hit the game's winning run.

Chuck was sharp and knew his audience well. He could recite the short falls of many gas station and restaurant bathrooms. He explained how his product was revolutionizing commercial bathrooms nationwide. To this day, I am convinced that if I owned a commercial building I don't think I would be able to sleep at night if I didn't have one of his products lined up for delivery to my place of business.

Value was Chuck's mantra. In fact, everything he said, did, or breathed about his product was all about value. He didn't talk about how long his company had been in business, or their state-of-art manufacturing equipment. Instead, he was well versed in what problems were frequently encountered by commercial properties as it related to tissue and towel supplies.

But it was more than knowing the problems; Chuck knew how to speak the language of commercial properties. He understood that their "sweet spots" were in reducing waste, decreasing costs, and improving efficiency. His value proposition went something like this:

"Much of towel and tissue waste is generated by 'in-a-hurry' patrons who use too much product. What my products can do for you is cut your paper

waste by X%, reduce your monthly costs by $Y, and improve the efficiency of your janitorial staff by Z man hours per week by providing an auto-stop function that dispenses only one paper towel at a time."

Chuck understood that it wasn't the products that his customers would buy, rather, it was the value that his products could bring to his customers. He used metrics - numbers, percentages and dollars - to clearly state the value in a measurable manner. Instead of just saying that he could cut paper waste, he made it crystal clear that customers who used his product could anticipate an X% cut in paper waste. The mere use of metrics not only helped to solidify his standing as an "expert" in his industry, but helped to demonstrate that he understood the problems impacting the average convenience store or gas station as it related to bathroom consumables.

Chuck knew how to make even the most hum-drum product seem like it was as life saving to a business as blood is to a transfusion patient. He not only understood his product line, but he knew his audience and how to catch their attention by identifying their most common needs and providing a solution to them.

. . .

Many sales-driven organizations believe that the way to effectively sell products or services is to talk about benefits, not features. For example, in the case of a salesperson selling mortgage loans the common feature-based statement used is, "Our loan programs come in three types: fixed, adjustable, and a conversion program."

However, it is more helpful for the customer to use a benefit-based statement such as, "The fixed option provides a stable payment with accelerated options for early payoff," or "The conversion program provides a low payment in the first 7 years to afford more home now."

What the client is hearing is stable payment, early payoff, low payment, and afford more home now. If any of these are of interest to the client, it opens them up to ask more questions so that you can help them get what they really want.

While selling benefits is far better than selling features, it still doesn't leverage your sales position. By far, the best method is to talk about clear and compelling value. In our example above, a value based statement would be, "On a $300,000 loan, our conversion program provides a savings of $4,100 in net out-of-pocket payments over the first two years as compared to today's national fixed rate average."

The difference in value-based selling is that you set the stage for the next question to be raised. The beauty in this is that the customer is actually doing all the work selling themselves, because they are hearing the value working with you, your product, etc. can bring to them.

In the legal world, attorneys are advised to never ask a question to which the answer is not known. This strategy offers them the ability to control what is being said without any surprises along the way.

The "ah" moment here is that by creating a pathway for your customers to immediately understand the value of your offer (whether it is a product or service), there is little resistance. This Client-Conscious approach simplifies the selling process because you are clearly breaking it down into the language of "value" which any client appreciates. Let me explain why.

When selling value, there are a variety of things which occur. First, you establish the trust of your prospect. They see that you not only understand their needs, but grasp how the value of your product or service could positively impact their overall situation. It then becomes a natural progression of conversation. The process looks something like this:

1) You initiate the contact and offer compelling value.

2) You are perceived as a trust-worthy source (or trusted advisor) who has a genuine interest in solving the problems or creating more opportunities for your prospect. (And, the bonus here is that you immediately differentiate yourself from all of your competitors who are using self-motivated pitches, while you are using customer-centric strategies!)

3) Because the prospects understand the value you bring, they are more willing to offer insight about what is really going on in their lives, and by having a better picture about what is truly going on...

4) You are able to offer a solution which you know matches their needs; which not only opens up the opportunity for them to...

5) Want to know more about your solution so you share with them feature and benefit statements.

6) You can create larger sales not only by serving more customers, but by finding the hidden sales opportunities that aren't typically uncovered in sales pitches!

BELIEF IS A RESULT OF PREPARATION

John Wooden the former men's basketball coach of the UCLA Bruins was named "Coach of the Century" by ESPN. His teams won an unprecedented ten national championships over the span of twelve years. During his coaching years, he was the consummate teacher with an empowering philosophy. In his book *Wooden*, the coach had this to say about his philosophy, "My thoughts were directed toward preparation, our journey, not the results of the effort (such as winning the national championship). That would have simply shifted my attention to the wrong area, hoping for something out of my control."

He added, "The journey is better than the inn [or destination]. I derived my greatest satisfaction out of the preparation - the 'journey.' The practice and planning and the drills were my journey and I loved it. A goal achieved is simply a by-product of all the hard work and good thinking you do along the way - your preparation. The preparation is where success is truly found." From the 'Coach of the Century,' we are reminded that success occurs on the practice field of life.

The preparation becomes easier and infinitely more effective in our sales career when we specialize in selling the value that we would buy.

> Identify what specific value excites you. What would you need to hear to create compelling reasons for you to buy?

Start by answering the question, "Why do people buy our product?" Get expert input from the wise people in your organization or ask existing customers if you can't come up with some solid answers to that question. (Often, the best place to go for those questions is your marketing department. These folks have a great deal of demographic research that, sadly, is rarely passed on to people in the sales department! By asking questions to the right people in your organization, you'll find yourself empowered with sales tools that you never imagined available.)

> A common reason for sales call reluctance is the salesperson's lack of belief in their product or service, and his or her inability to convey how it could help the prospective customer

When you are armed with the information about why people buy your products or services, then personalize it by determining: "What are the most beneficial aspects of my product as they relate to my life? As a potential customer of my product what would make me buy it?" This is where preparation and professionalism meet as a success strategy.

Identify what specific value excites you. What would you need to hear to create compelling reasons for you to buy? Some common values include: cutting costs, saving time, increasing productivity, decreasing turn-over, reducing waste, improving revenue, and so forth. Personalize value as individual stories experienced by you or others from your life and share this real-life enthusiasm. Case studies from existing clients can be extremely helpful in understanding the problems which were identified, the solutions you offered, and the value you brought to the customer.

Donald Trump was quoted as saying, "You must believe in what you sell to make a profit." Commonly, sales call reluctance is due to the salesperson's lack of belief in his/her product or service, and his or her inability to convey how it could help the prospective customer. Forced enthusiasm comes across and is the sure-fire sign of an inexperienced salesperson.

Client-Conscious Salespeople find much of their success coming from the initial preparation they "put in" at the beginning. It was found in learning what excited them about their products value and creating personal stories and experiences. What they do from there is simply tell the stories of value by conveying these experiences with the top three or so value statements that would appeal to their client.

I liken this approach to a professional singer who cuts a hit song. The song is well-received, people "buy it" because they like it - it serves a purpose and benefits them. Ten years later, the hit song is still popular with the fans because they still like it. They like it so much they go to see the singer in concert to hear her music, but especially for that particular song. In actuality, they are still "buying" it because it still works, it still benefits them.

Now here is where the professionalism comes in. Throughout the ten years since the song came out, she has practiced and delivered these lyrics thousands of times. And the professional singer still sings it the original way because it works. The fans are still "buying" and still benefiting. The Client- Conscious Salesperson will find those "hits" which are simply their product's success stories - the ones they believe in - and they'll repeat those same stories and value statements over and over, year in and year out until they are not only committed to memory but could recite them in their sleep. For this is what their prospects buy year in and year out.

> An enthusiastic belief is developed through preparation.

It simplifies the selling process for the salesperson because they become "specialists" in these three or so value statements.

The prepared salesperson has belief in his/her product or service which comes across as a natural enthusiasm. Remember old Chuck Munroe, he exuded this enthusiasm and made anyone within ear shot get excited about, of all things... toilet paper!

Enthusiastic belief is not something that comes when we are hired or even trained by the company who employs us. We have to work for it! An enthusiastic belief is developed through preparation. Develop this skill of "selling the value that you would buy" and you will possess that rare attribute of natural enthusiasm.

SELL THE VALUE THAT YOU WOULD BUY

- Understand all the reasons why people buy your company's products/services.

- Based upon the feedback you receive about why people buy, create a short list of the three to five most compelling reasons that would make you buy your product/service.

- Develop metrics that are based on true stories of what your product/service does on the average in the marketplace that coincide with each compelling reason. (E.g. it decreases waste by 30% and increases overall revenue by 10% over a 12 month period.)

- Using these compelling reasons and metrics, paint pictures in the prospects minds of them living with the "sweet spot" value that they desire most. Reinforce this value with true stories from your experience and the experience of others benefiting as you believe they will if they use your product or service.

Client-Conscious Prospecting™

Chapter 4

Ask For Help and
Then Take It

Chapter 4

ASK FOR HELP

AND THEN TAKE IT

> You must be
> willing to
> receive the
> help

Salespeople are like any other people in that they see the world through their own perspective or "belief" filter. This filter has been developed from real-world experiences as well as our own beliefs about what we think will (or won't) work. Even if we are not getting the sales results we desire, it is easy to stay with what we've been doing and believing that with more time and/or more effort, things will change for the better.

Frank Sinatra would have liked the selling profession. As sales professionals, we find comfort in doing it "our way." For some of us we keep repeating the same sales techniques, no matter what company we work for or what products or services we sell.

When prospecting results are not generating the kinds of success we desire, it is time to take a different course of action. Simply because the method you are comfortable using has become habit doesn't mean that it is the best or most effective. A principle for top performance is to learn to ask for help and then be willing (and consciously able) to accept the help that is offered to you.

Successful people are successful for a reason; they have uncovered the secret to success. Ask them what they do, do what they do, and you'll get similar results. This requires a conscious change in the way we think and behave because as humans not only do we resist change but we find comfort in the safety of what is known to us. By asking successful people for help, we are allowing them to give, which in turn helps them to take part in the prosperous cycle of conscious living.

In helping you succeed, these successful individuals succeed at an even greater level. It is how the world works. When you believe that you are actually giving (instead of believing you are imposing by asking questions), you are initiating the rewards for both parties which are a win/win for everyone.

You are success-worthy. How you can prove this out in the world is that you ask for help from the people who can help you succeed. It's not enough, however to ask for help, you must be willing to receive the help. The key to your success is to ask, accept, and act.

I wonder how many millionaires/billionaires through the years would have gladly mentored others if they just had been asked!

When we find it in ourselves to ask for the help from the right people and then act on this help, what can follow is a new way of doing business that can have far reaching benefits. Stop doing what you've been doing by abandoning the old and accepting the new.

The successful people in your company are the ones getting the specific results you desire most. It's important to be clear on who you want to be contacting for advice and insight to ensure that your mentor mirrors your ideals. For example, if you want to double your income while working a maximum of 40 hours per week, your best mentor is not a seven figure salesperson who is working 80 hours a week to achieve the goal. Instead, find the top producer who is living the life you desire and have a conversation with him or her, remembering that successful people will help you. Like much in life, the gift is there for you to take it, but you must be willing to ask, accept it, and then act on what you have learned.

. . .

Years ago, I had the good fortune to have an office right next to the top producing salesperson for the Fortune 100 bank which employed us both. Her name was Debbie, and she was a winner in both sales and in her life objectives. Over a few years we developed a friendship which included long talks on sales techniques as well as life techniques.

Debbie had a powerful approach to life and was passionate about living it to its fullest. The thing I'll never forget she said was that success is a "mindset." It's a "knowing that I belong" attitude. I have learned that this "I belong" attitude is developed through experience, not through logical understanding.

There can be no substitute for direct, hands on experience. Direct experience is what creates the "I belong here" attitude. It is what separates the rookie from the veteran in the affairs of life itself.

My "I belong here" experience came as a gift wrapped in barbed wire. At the time, I had developed some relationships with real estate offices in my area. One such office was looking for a financial sponsor to help support a regional awards breakfast. Two hundred of the top realtors were to receive recognition for their sales production for the previous year.

I had suggested to my management that we should be a financial sponsor, which involved a $1000 contribution in exchange for a publicity opportunity for our company. The publicity I explained, would be a 20 minute speech explaining the home loan process from an inside perspective as well as selling our company's benefits/reasons to do business with us.

My company was willing to make the financial investment but wanted a loan consultant to give the speech. What surprised me was that the loan consultant they wanted to speak was me!

Filled with a hundred forms of self-doubt, I reluctantly gave the presentation. My fear of failure kicked in yet I committed to both a national real estate chain and my own company as well. My professional reputation was at stake. It is here where life gave me a positive shot in the arm. For within 90 days of giving the presentation my business exploded.

The short 20 minute presentation had given me instant credibility with the top real estate professionals in my area. Much more importantly, I realized that I was the knowledgeable expert in my field that my referral sources needed and would be depending upon for future sales. I came face to face with the realization that if I didn't believe that I was qualified to be the expert, my clients and referral sources wouldn't believe in me either.

The moral of this is that I could have given affirmations as to my value to the market place until I was blue in the face and still lived with reluctant fear. It was however, direct experience that "showed" me that I belong. The regret I had then was that I always had "belonged," I just didn't believe it.

One of my sales goals included succeeding in the "high end client" marketplace. As luck would have it, one of the highest paid sales consultants in the United States worked out of the Boca Raton office, just 25 miles north of where I lived. I had never met John before but his reputation preceded him. He was a legend in the company. Everyone wanted to know his secrets, including me. John was considered the most savvy sales consultant in the company because he only closed deals larger than a million dollars. He clearly had mastered the arena which provided the most lucrative payouts.

If the truth be told, at the time I was nervous to call him. Wild thoughts rolled through my mind, expecting that John probably wouldn't have much time to chat with me. I was pleasantly surprised when John answered the phone. I told him that my intent was to achieve similar results and asked if he would help me.

John was gracious and offered his strategies, thoughts, and techniques over the course of our call. At the end of the conversation, which I found extremely valuable, he said, "I appreciate your call. I don't get calls like this much, it's been a pleasure."

What was reinforced that day was that successful people really are willing to help. They just need to be asked. It's no surprise that most of us aren't maximizing our full potential because we don't allow others, who are more successful, the opportunity to give of their time and wisdom.

One of the things John mentioned during my conversation with him was this, "Success in this business is all about how you see yourself. Do you see yourself as one who belongs with the big fish or not? That's the difference!" It was then that I realized that in order to see myself belonging with the big fish, I needed to at least start swimming in their pond.

> Success in this business is all about how you see yourself

Building on the techniques that I learned from both Debbie and John, I created my own, personalized prospecting approach. I started by identifying more than 10 high payoff prospecting techniques used by these top producers. Then, I customized my prospecting approach to fit within my own personal style and strengths by specializing in only three techniques and I went deep. I utilized a combination of methods - a direct mail campaign, public speaking as a prospecting tool, and creating a "golden referral base" of qualified business allies as my sales plan. I maintained the Client-Conscious Prospecting™ approach and I got busy, real busy.

Of course adapting my style of selling to a higher payoff approach took some time. I hyper-focused these techniques to my target market. In the end, there was no guess work when it came to prospecting. I had a clear agenda and plan that I needed to complete week in and week out. Over time, business far surpassed my expectations. I was annually recognized for top sales production by my company and became a "specialist" in this large client arena - something I had wanted to do for quite some time.

But what was really amazing was that the process was simple, and painless. It did require work and time, but the process itself was a no-brainer.

You can achieve your goals! Start by asking for help and then eagerly accept it when it is offered to you. It really couldn't be more simple.

ASK, ACCEPT, AND ACT

You may wonder, "How do I initiate my own success?" The process is simple. Start by identifying three people who are achieving the goals you want most. Consider not only the goals they are achieving in their professional lives, but the kind of lifestyle they live outside of the office setting. Then, once you've identified them, it's time to find out specifically what they are doing to get those consistent results. The best way to understand how they have obtained success is to interview them and ask specific, open-end questions which elicit detailed answers.

Remember, you are on a mission to uncover the specific high payoff techniques that will deliver what you desire, or better still, exceed your expectations. Keep in mind that the techniques you discover will help to form your action plan, so the more detailed you can get, the more information you will have to establish your winning strategy.

If you are lucky enough to have a good relationship with top performers already, then it should be even easier to ask them for help. Often, however, top performers are high profile people in your company that you don't know. But have no fear. Remember, you are on a journey to find your key to success so embrace the opportunities to meet new people and learn from them.

Start the process by calling these successful performers and introducing yourself. A good script to use is the following:

Hi ____, I'm (state your name and your industry) **and we haven't met yet** (confident, yet honest posture), **but I'm appreciative of your work and the results you are getting. I'd like to learn how to get similar results myself. I believe I have the right desire, but I've lacked the ability to ask for help from the people who have the experience I lack** (shows your vulnerability). **I could sure use your help.**

Would it be possible to spend 20 - 30 minutes (position it as a real meeting) **with you over a meal or the phone?**

(Remember, it may take a few weeks for them to clear a spot in their calendar, but it will be worth the wait!)

<u>End the call</u> (regardless of outcome).

I'm thankful for your time and look forward to: (select one, as applicable)

• Appointment set

(Our appointment on <u>DATE</u> at <u>TIME</u>)

• Follow up set

(Following up with you on <u>DATE</u>)

• Decline of your request

(Our paths crossing again sometime)

<u>Questions</u>

Keeping things simple during your "interview" with a top performer is important. In the spirit of simplifying the process, the following questions can provide the nuts and bolts of strategy for you to create your own action plan.

a.) What two actions have made the greatest contribution to your results?

b.) What are the three most important things that you would recommend I do to get similar results?

c.) Are there any people/businesses that you would recommend I contact that can help me?

Success is hardly an individual effort. As the adage goes, "it takes a village." Recognizing that there is enough for everyone to have a piece of the sales action will help considerably in

> Success is hardly an individual effort. As the adage goes, "it takes a village."

finding strategic partners and alliances to build your business contacts. In strengthening our relationship building skills, we extend an opportunity for others to contribute to us. Obviously, the more they contribute to us, the more we are willing to contribute to them. It becomes the law of cause and effect.

When you are specific with your questions, it will be appreciated because it demonstrates that you are prepared and solution-oriented. Also, it causes the person you are interviewing to hyper-focus on the key result areas that have helped him or her succeed. If these questions don't get to the heart of what you need to know, then use these questions as a starting point to create your own questions. The key is to be specific and keep it simple with just a few well-thought questions.

By asking questions that are critical to uncovering high payoff techniques and strategies, you have just unlocked the door to expert guidance from someone who has achieved exactly what you want. The Client-Conscious salesperson will ask for help from the right people therefore learning new success techniques. This information is priceless, so use it to your advantage!

ASK FOR HELP AND THEN TAKE IT

- Identify three people who are getting the exact result you want and interview them, asking:

1. What two actions have made the greatest contribution to your results?

2. What are the three most important things that you would recommend I do to get similar results?

3. Are there any people/businesses that you would recommend I contact that can help me?

4. Is there anything else you would recommend to me that could help me reach my production / work goal?

- From this information, determine what fits your strengths and interests and formulate your Client-Conscious Prospecting™ plan and get to work.

Client-Conscious Prospecting™

Chapter 5
Exert Your Success
Worthiness

Chapter 5

EXERT YOUR

SUCCESS WORTHINESS

> We are always
> worthy of
> the best

Success is a mindset. In fact, the best athletes in the world have recognized that having an "I belong here attitude" is what catapults their professional athletic careers. How you see yourself will determine whether or not you play in the big arenas in life. As the proverb goes, "Think big for bigger results. Think small and you will always play small."

Prospecting with confidence comes directly from the inner worthiness that each of us possesses. We just need to take the extra effort to believe we belong in the big leagues!

A person's inner belief system will dictate how far one is willing to go to assert himself/herself in asking for business. Dreaming and goal attainment are good, but I have found that many goals/dreams go unclaimed because of an inability to exert success worthiness.

Have you been the person in your life that has been your own best critic? For most of us, we're our own worst enemy! We sabotage our success with feelings of inadequacy and inferiority. This lack of confidence is only magnified because we replay the negative thoughts, attitudes, and beliefs until we actually believe in them.

Our minds are extremely powerful. But thankfully, we have the power (and the ability) to determine what information we choose to believe!

We can stop the cycle of unhealthy thoughts and beliefs by focusing on helping someone else.

Think good thoughts toward your prospects. Find ways to help that client who is in most need.

Not only does focusing on someone else's needs help to free you from your natural self-centered tendencies, but it also helps us boost our confidence. Ponder for a moment the last time you did something special for someone. How did you feel afterwards?

Think about that for a moment. You have the ability to do things for others all day long and to feel the sense of ease that comes with helping someone else.

If you put your sole focus on helping a person you encounter on your next sales call, how do you think you might be received? This is the essence of Client-Conscious Prospecting™. It's impossible to be in fear when we are helping someone because we are not thinking of ourselves. When we think and act right toward others, we are brought back in balance to our inherent worthiness to receive.

There's a theme throughout this book that started with the concept of **The Shift** in Chapter 1 and has continued to this point. The information contained in this chapter is the most critical element in a salesperson's success. It separates the person who is comfortable around high self-image people and ones who aren't. Our self-consciousness creates fear and self-doubt. However, a Client-Consciousness immediately gives us that "personal power" needed to approach anyone, anytime, anywhere in any market segment. This is because our motives are sound.

> The word *deserve* in Latin means to be "of service." To be "of service" is a key to feeling worthy of success and deserving of the good things in life.

We are always worthy of the best. It's not possible for someone else to affect our worthiness. That's an inside job. Individually, each of us is responsible for how we think and respond with action. We "think small" with negative thoughts or actions directed at ourselves or others, and diminish our "perception" of our own worthiness. By doing this, we lose our power, but once again, it's an inside job.

There are countless examples in life of people engaging in destructive behaviors because at a root level they feel they don't deserve (or aren't worthy) of a better life. This behavior is self-motivated because of negative and unhealthy inner beliefs. Beliefs are what control actions, which is why negative thoughts lead to destructive (even on a small scale) actions. Whether these beliefs are true or false doesn't matter, we act from them anyway.

In life, we get what we think we deserve. If we hoard our gifts and time, and beat ourselves up with feelings of self-criticism we are creating a negative "cause." The "effect" that follows is an inner feeling that we don't deserve the best, whether at a conscious or subconscious level, and we act from this belief.

Our beliefs are acted out in the world in many ways. Fear of failure, self-sabotage, and fear of asking for what we want all lead us to avoid stepping out of our comfort zone and exploring newer (and often better) opportunities. We are left asking for less than we could have had and tend to feel uncomfortable around highly confident people.

There's a life lesson here. The word deserve in Latin means to be "of service." To be "of service" is a key to feeling worthy of success and deserving of the good things in life. A direct way of increasing our success worthiness is by being of service. This makes us feel we deserve (consciously or sub-consciously) so we believe it and we act from this belief. The ripple in one's life begins as soon as the thought or action is taken.

Two of the greatest sales people in history are Mother Teresa and Dr. Martin Luther King. While neither of them were sales people by profession, they had the courage to ask the world to change for the better. Through criticism and scorn, they fearlessly prospected for the causes they believed in and asked the world to join them in making positive changes. The world did change as a result of their efforts.

Neither of these leaders in social change were perfect; after all, they were as human as you and me. However, they took a stand on specific life changing issues and gained strength through their service. They held a genuine worthiness that people admired and followed.

In the CareerTrack audio program "21 Days to Self-Discovery," author Carol Price tells of a survey she conducted years before of several thousand people who were asked this question:

Find a person in your life that represents these three issues:

1.) The person who has recognized your value more than anyone else has.

2.) The person who sees your potential more than anyone else has.

3.) The person who supports you better than anyone else has.

The result of thousands of participants revealed this telling conclusion: Only 8% used their own name for all three. Eight percent of a large sampling of people actually take responsibility for their own empowerment.

> In life, we get what we think we deserve

We can choose to be victims to our own selfish need for recognition from others, or we can tap into the flow of prosperity by contributing to another's well being thereby increasing our inner worthiness and earning the peace and prosperity we desire and seek. Practice the Client-Conscious Prospecting™ approach by exerting your success worthiness today.

EXERT YOUR SUCCESS WORTHINESS

- In life, we get what we think we deserve.

- Let go of selfish, self-centered thoughts and concentrate on the best interests of others. In doing so, your self esteem will increase. The great equalizer is selflessness because it brings balance back to our inherent worthiness to receive what the world (and others) have to offer us.

- A direct way to increase our success worthiness is by being of service. This makes us feel we deserve, so we believe it and we act from this belief. It's positive karma, and its effect is immediate. The ripple in one's life begins as soon as the thought or action is taken.

- Make the answer to these three statements - **YOU:**

    1. The person who has recognized your value more than anyone else has.

2. The person who sees your potential more than anyone else has.

3. The person who supports you better than anyone else has.

Client-Conscious Prospecting™

Conclusion:

The Parable of the Client-Conscious Salesperson

CONCLUSION

The Parable of the
Client-Conscious Salesperson

Shane was sitting in the last row of the plane headed for the South Pacific to the island owned by the prestigious company who employed him. This was his first President's Club trip, a week-long vacation provided by his company for only the company's top sales producers.

Even though his company paid for family members to come along, Shane and his wife Maggie agreed that with both of their children's school and upcoming exam schedule, it wouldn't be the right time to miss a whole week of school. So, Shane soloed the flight, promising to hurry back home.

As the plane prepared for take-off, Shane reflected back just a few hours when he was leaving the house.

"You have our full support. Go have fun; you've earned it and try to relax," Maggie said as she leaned over and kissed him on the cheek. She didn't mention to him that she had been worried about the long hours he spent at work, or that he was missing time away from the girls. "Oh," she continued, handing him an envelope. "I forgot to give these pictures to you. They're for you to look at on your flight."

In that instant, Shane remembered the envelope and where he had placed it in one of his carry-on bags. He opened the envelope. Inside, there were several crayon drawings. One in particular contained an illustration of a stick figure with a tired and frowning face. "Daddy" scrawled across the top in bright red crayon.

There were several letters from Shane's children also inside, "Daddy, we love you. We miss you," the letters read.

As Shane poured through the papers and looked at the photos of his smiling children and his beautiful wife, tears started streaming down his face.   After putting the envelope back in his briefcase, he sat confused taking an inventory of his situation.

Eight years with his company, he thought. Steady sales increase each year. With each year came more hours, more stress, less time for himself and his family. Strong income - no lifestyle!

This "vacation" was his first President's club reward. It should have been a time to celebrate, bask in the glory, and relax. Yet Shane sat misty-eyed feeling depressed, burnt out, and exhausted. He didn't feel like celebrating. As he projected to the week after the vacation's end, he was filled with anxiety that he'd have to get at it again. After all, the company and his family depended on him.

What Shane wouldn't share with anyone, not even Maggie, was that he felt unsure of himself on a weekly basis. His stomach sank every time he had to go out and prospect a new contact. He was anxious at the very thought of how he would be received and felt an underlying tension that lasted even when he wasn't at work. "I'm a top producer now, I shouldn't feel this way," he thought, with an underlying anger directed toward himself.

The reality of the situation was that Shane had been unhappy at work for some time. Seeing the drawing from his daughters merely offered a visual affirmation that he was miserable, and symbolized the guilt he felt about his imbalanced life. He felt guilty when thinking about his personal life - missed recitals, missed bedtime stories, missed school plays.

Each sales rep had his own row of five seats on the chartered plane. Shane noticed in the row in front of him sat the top salesperson in the company. Perched comfortably by the window sat 57 year-old Cade Caldwell. It was fitting that Cade sat with his head leaning against the window, looking as if he was ready for an enjoyable week. After all, Cade was known throughout the company as "Mr. Relaxed."

Cade had been with the company for twenty years, and in that time he was by far the top salesperson nationwide each year. He was an enjoyable one to talk with; the kind of guy you could let your guard down with and be yourself. His demeanor was jovial, as he seemed to always walk around with a look on his face like he was holding back a really good joke.

Shane heard of "Mr. Relaxed" and often wondered what made him so successful at such a young age. Cade had produced enough sales for the company each year that it paid him more than anyone in the company, including the CEO.

Shane noticed that Cade, too, was traveling without his family. "Oh, she's flying in on Tuesday," Shane had overheard Cade tell a flight attendant when asked about his wife.

As Shane reflected on his life, he couldn't help but wonder what it would be like to know how this wealthy man attained the lifestyle he was living.

"His limited work schedule and personal lifestyle is a thing of dreams," Shane remembered his sales manager Warren saying on more than one occasion. "If you ever get the chance to ask him how he conducts his business, listen to every word because in my 42 years in selling I've never seen or heard of anyone who did it better."

Over the course of the next hour, Shane became consumed with the thought that Cade might have something to share with him that could change his life. Shane's inner conversation kept telling him to make the contact but as soon as he thought of taking the action he was filled with fear.

The internal conversation continued, "This guy is a multi-millionaire, a legend in the industry. Who am I to be asking him for help?" Shane's fear kept him in his chair.

Lucky for him the voice inside his head said, "Get up. Go talk to Cade. What do you have to lose?" Shane was suddenly met with a conviction that he knew what he had to do. He unfastened his seat belt, slowly stood up and then proceeded to sit down next to Cade Caldwell and open up dialogue.

"Mr. Caldwell, I'm Shane Nicks from our Palm Valley office."

Mr. Relaxed said, "Please, call me Cade. Mr. Caldwell was my father."

Both men chuckled a moment as Cade continued, "Shane I've seen your numbers. You've done some good work this year."

Shane opened, "It's my first time in the President's Club after eight years of giving this job my all. The result is that I've never been so highly paid and yet so highly miserable in my entire life."

Cade smiled, as he nodded his head. "Yes. I can see the exhaustion on your face."

Shane then said, "Cade, can I be honest with you?"

"Actually, it's the very thing I appreciate in people the most. Please, what's on your mind?" inquired Cade.

"Well," started Shane nervously, "I am hoping for things to change... and soon. I just can't keep this up, I'm burnt out. I look at you, and see a guy who doesn't seem burdened like me and the other sales reps. I've noticed even the performers who look happy, upon closer analysis are just as miserable as me. They just have better "masking" abilities to hide their frustration. I don't know what to do, but I know that I can't keep doing what I'm doing... it's too exhausting."

Cade patiently listened, nodding his head ever so slightly.

"Cade, I'm wondering, can you help me?

Mr. Relaxed smiled a long smile, "I've worked for this company for twenty years and you are the very first sales representative who has actually had the gut level honesty to admit to me that your way isn't working. I admire this in you, Shane, more than you know. I'd be delighted to help."

Shane felt a sudden sense of relief... and a bit of excitement as Cade continued, "What I know about change in my own life is that it wasn't until I had a compelling 'why' that gave me the open mind needed to do something different. Sometimes that 'why' is pain. I know it doesn't seem like it, but that misery you are feeling now could be a great gift. Some people get bogged down in the tough times, not being patient enough to find the message."

Looking Shane directly in the eye, Cade paused before stating, "For the first 20 years of my selling career, my day was all about what I could get. I planned my week before it started. I planned each day before it started. I bullied through my fears and gave everything to my work. As a result, I was in the top 20% of sales performers. I had achieved a goal I had always desired to accomplish."

"I went through some really hard times, yet my family stuck by me. I provided a good living for them was my rationalization. Yet I worked long hours, sacrificed weekends and evenings, and missed more of my kid's school and sporting events than I care to admit to. Truth be told, there wasn't much of me left to give to my family when I got home. I was exhausted, and this pattern translated into a household of 'Dad's tired' or 'Dad's grumpy.' "

"I can relate," said Shane, remembering the crayon picture still in his carry-on bag.

Cade continued, "Selling the way I sold was absolutely exhausting. I prospected to the masses. I dreaded the prospecting process, every bit of it, for 20 years. I felt the anxiety in my chest when I was about to initiate the call. The warm flashes I experienced when I knew that the prospect knew when I was trying to convince them to buy. I lived in discomfort not knowing what next month would bring and wondered constantly - am I doing enough?"

"One day I came to a crossroads in my career. By that, I mean I was so confused and burnt out that I couldn't muster the motivation to even go out on a sales call. I knew I was in trouble, but had no idea what to do about it. For the fourth day in a row, I went to the beach instead of going to work, and walked mile after sand covered mile deep in thought."

"On the fourth day, I walked past the town's carnival-on-the-beach, complete with a ferris wheel. As I walked by, I waved to the smiling ticket taker named Roy. He had worked at the carnival for at least the 15 or so years we had been bringing our children to the beach amusement park. He seemed like a happy-go-lucky kind of a guy. Mid-seventies, medium build with a head of deep white hair. He always dressed impeccably and one could tell he took pride in his appearance."

"As I mentioned, I was more confused and despondent than I had been all week. Walking by I said to him, 'Roy, I've been coming here for years with my kids and every time, without fail, I've seen you here checking people in with a peace about you that I admire. For the past week, I've walked by each day to see your smiling face and I've wondered how you can keep such a relaxed demeanor about you.' "

"'Roy,' I said. 'My life is a mess. I don't have the guts to go back to my sales job. I'm burnt out and can't keep calling on people because I'm expecting them to reject me. I don't know why I'm telling you all of this. Maybe because I remember one of my children saying that you were a man who loves it when the park visitors are having a good time.' "

" 'You seem so happy in your work day after day, year after year. I'm struggling in my life and just can't seem to figure my way out of it, but I know something's got to change. Roy, can you help me?' "

"Sitting in the ticket booth, Roy's eyebrows lifted in amazement as he said, 'What did you say?' Roy stood up, opened the back door of the booth and stood face to face with me as he said again, 'What did you say?' "

Shane was hooked on Cade's story. It was getting good. He listened intently as Cade's story unfolded.

"'Hey, I'm sorry I ruffled your feathers. Forget it, I guess I asked the wrong person for help,' I said. 'No, no no...' stammered Roy, 'Let me assure you that you have asked the right person. I've been living with a mental treasure for years, wanting others to experience but had never been asked. I'd be delighted to help you.' "

" 'What you have just asked me shows the readiness to receive which is needed to change your circumstances. You are fortunate son, you may not see it now, but you are fortunate indeed. My life changed as the result of a shift in how I viewed my life. When I was in my twenties, I had a similar experience to what you are going through presently. I was trying to make sense of my life and bounced from job to job because I was never really good at business or anything else for that matter. In a desperate moment I called my grandfather and asked him for help just as you have done here today with me.' "

" 'My grandfather was the happiest man I ever met. He always seemed to be at ease in his life. In addition he was comfortable financially. He loved cooking and owned a well-known restaurant in New York City where he was proprietor and chef. The stock market collapse lead to his restaurant going bankrupt. But within three years, he was back in business which remained highly successful until his passing about 20 years ago. He loved to cook and enjoy his patron's pleasure in experiencing his finished product.' "

" 'My grandfather shared with me a mental approach to business that he said was the greatest lesson he had ever learned. It allowed him to be magnificently successful in the very things that brought him his most joy - cooking and service. He called this great lesson *the shift* and said it was passed down from his great grandfather who incidentally worked as a public servant in Washington D.C. for the Lincoln Administration.' "

Cade stopped for a moment, and looked at Shane. "Roy told me that this simple lesson applied in his life allowed him to not only get out of his slump, but to experience a life-long dream himself. He said that the happiest times in his childhood were when he worked as a merry-go round operator at the fair in his hometown. He said that he never got tired of being at a fair, he could do it day in and day out with the same joy and gratification. This was his 'bliss' he said."

"To my surprise, Roy said that he had owned the carnival-on-the-beach for some thirty years. The principle shared by his grandfather helped him to succeed in... of all things... selling, which became so lucrative that he retired at 42 and bought the amusement park. He said that his joy never dwindled because there are new people at the park every day so he was able to experience their laughter and excitement along with them."

"Now, are you ready for the best part of this story?" Cade questioned Shane. Shane nodded in agreement.

"Roy reached into his pocket and handed me a card which contained a one sentence explanation of this shift with some brief instructions. Roy then shook my hand, wished me well, and then went back to his ticket booth."

"If I didn't believe in miracles up until that point in my life, I sure did after that day," said Cade. "What led me to the beach? Why did I open up to a man who I've said less than ten words to... in the fifteen years that I'd been acquainted with him? This man was in possession of the very thing that I was looking for, yet I had no idea whatsoever that I was looking for it."

"So," Shane interrupted Cade, "What did the card say?" Shane felt like a little child waiting to get to the end of a good book.

"Well," continued Cade, slowly. "I read this card over and over for at least a week to figure out how I could employ this gift that was so well promoted by Roy. Finally, I connected with how I could use it in my own career. From that day forward, I let go of my old and stressful way of selling and changed my approach."

"I started by getting out to help ten people a week solve problems in their business life. Past clients, prospects, sideline businesses. I even worked with business people who were actually vendors for our company. It didn't necessarily have to be direct prospects for our product."

"By giving of myself, those around me were able to experience the best part of me. And that was my gift. I was able to feel good by helping them and expecting nothing in return."

Cade stopped for a moment. The silence was golden. "Shane," Cade said in a low voice, "That's how trust is built. Do you think they remember me and what I do when interacting with their spheres of influence?"

"Back then, I was helping a little more than 40 people per month, about 500 people per year. Be it a consultant, an advisor, a referral source – whatever they needed - I became their trusted business ally. My job was to take the time on even the seemingly 'unproductive' people by helping them in ways that clearly would not directly result in increased business for me."

"When I followed this process as a business philosophy, something came over me that changed me in a way that made me more attractive to people. People seemed to be more open with me without knowing me for long."

"Kind of like I'm doing right now, huh?" Shane said.

"Precisely, Shane, and it's still something I don't completely understand, but I don't worry about it. I began to 'lighten up' and relax for probably the first time in my adult life. As a salesperson, I became sort of 'fearless.' "

Shane chuckled as he imagined Cade in a cape and leotards. He could almost see Cade as the super hero of salespeople. The image was amusing.

But Cade continued, unaware of Shane's mental picture. "What's the number one thing we fear as salespeople?" said Cade.

"Initiating the contact... making the initial sales call," answered Shane.

"And who is that fear about?" inquired Cade.

"Us," said Shane.

"Ah, so you are starting to see it," said Cade as he smiled. "But if we are focused on helping a prospect... who are we thinking about?"

"Them," said Shane.

"So if we are thinking about them, then we are not thinking about ourselves, right?" Cade said while looking directly into Shane's eyes making sure he was following.

Knowing that he had Shane's full attention, Cade continued, "Do you know that if we are not thinking of ourselves we cannot experience fear. It's one of the universal success truths for wealthy living."

"There is an Attraction Law that can simplify a whole lot for us in life if we just use it correctly. It states that each one of us attracts the people and circumstances in our lives through our dominant thoughts and feelings. Bringing this into the selling profession here's what I discovered: If our dominant thoughts are on how can I maximize my sales... in essence we are motivated by greed, selling becomes a battle. With this as our dominant thoughts, our motivation is 'selfish.' which then attracts and brings out the selfishness in others."

"What we are doing is attracting resistance from others. It makes selling a grind. This is what I did for the first 20 years of my selling career. Right out of high school I began selling, and all I did was attract rejection after rejection. Even clients who needed my product would haggle with me all day long to get the best deal they could regardless of how it affected me, my company, or the next client who might come along. I felt beat up even after I made a sale."

Shane interrupted, "Let me make sure I understand. What you are saying is that as salespeople we bring out or attract the very same attitude in others that we are projecting from within ourselves."

"You got it, Shane, you've known this all your life. But, our inner selfish needs push back this fact and it takes times like these to move the knowledge back into our conscious state so we can use them," said Cade.

Visibly connecting to the conversation Shane continued, "So if I decide to place my thoughts on helping others and that's my motivation, then within them will come an instinctive desire to help me in some way. Is that correct?" Shane asked inquisitively.

"If not from them, it will come from someone else or in another way completely unknown to you. It's impossible to figure this stuff out, I've stopped trying," offered Cade.

"In every case, by doing this you've earned trust and created a karmic turn in the world. What goes around Shane... really does come around! My old philosophy kept me bound in thinking that I was never doing enough. I had declining health, an estranged family, and an emptiness inside that I wouldn't wish on anyone."

"Today, I'm 57 years of age and I work 25 hours a week about 10 months a year. I spend more time with my wife, children, and grandchildren than most retired people. As a family, we own six community centers for at-risk teenage children in our home state. Each center serves children from low income families to ultra-wealthy families. I've come to find that at-risk is not limited just to the inner-city."

"Along with sporting and enrichment activities, we teach the very universal truth I'm explaining to you now. I golf each week, walk every day with my wife and our dog Max, and have plenty of time to compete in aqua-thons."

"Shane, the reason why I produce the numbers I do each year in such little working hours is that I've embraced what I am. I'm a salesperson and my role is to prospect for new business. There is no other position within our company that is paid to do this... it's our job. They actually rely on us to be as good as we can be at this one skill."

"What I see many of our sales brethren doing is they try to do everything. I know, I used to do it myself. They are doing all of their own paperwork. They are creating their own marketing flyers. They spend time in clerical matters and other duties that are better suited for someone with that skill set. A third of their week or more is completely wasted. They just haven't connected with what our 'role' is as salespeople. Sadly, many of them actually prefer to do these low payoff tasks because it allows them to avoid prospecting which, for them, is the most painful part of their week."

"Henry Ford found that his success came from surrounding himself with people wiser than he and bringing their efforts together into value for the marketplace."

"Wow, that's profound," said Shane.

Continued Cade, "As a rule, I do very little of my own paperwork. I could, but it would be a low-payoff behavior. My assistant Kaye is exceptional at streamlining the paperwork. I review it before submission, but that's all I do with it. For marketing purposes, I enlist the help of companies on a per project basis. I make about a 4,000% margin of increased sales compared to my direct cost. All of the industry articles that are authored by me have come from my 'in the trenches' research on needs directly from my clients. I provide that material to a 'contract writer,' and they pump out professionally written articles that educate our customers and build credibility for me."

"I spend most of my time in the highest payoff activity of all: prospecting for new business. I do this with a mental approach that builds trust quickly and naturally leads to business in ways I couldn't have possibly predicted."

"With this shift in place, I act daily on my ability to prospect anyone, anytime, in any market segment. Today, I have no reluctance or fear prospecting anyone because a success worthiness has been developed within me as a result of making this shift in attitude."

Cade's conversation had been so interesting that neither Cade nor Shane were aware of how much time had passed until the beep from the seatbelt sign went off overhead.

Cade reached into his suitcase and grabbed a small gold plated index card. Holding it in his right hand he said, "Twenty years ago, I was given this message and was told to pass it on only to people who directly ask for help from me. In my career with this company, you are the very first and I'm honored to give you this," said Cade as he handed Shane the card.

Before Shane could look at its content, Cade put his hand on his right shoulder and said, "I'll ask of you the same that was asked of me. Pass it on to people who ask you for help. Don't ever sell this message. Just provide it when there's a sincere person in your life willing to ask."

Shane nodded his head and then thanked Cade. The men shook hands, and Cade exited the plane. Holding this new gift in his hands, Shane read the inscription on the card:

WITHIN EACH DAY, FOCUS YOUR

MENTAL APPROACH ON

FURTHERING THE INTERESTS

OF THE PEOPLE YOU SERVE

INDEPENDENT OF ANY DIRECT

PERSONAL BENEFIT

- THE SHIFT

After pondering it's content, Shane gathered up his bags, exited the plane, and then found a seat where he could reflect back on his conversation with Mr. Relaxed.

The gate doors were still open. The plane was still docked. Shane didn't hesitate. He stood up and walked to the plane asking the two pilots, "Are you headed back to home base now?"

The senior pilot in the left seat said, "Yeah, going back to get round two of you guys right after we get gassed up and pass inspection."

Shane said, "Great, I'd like to fly back if it's all the same to you. I just realized where I want to be for the next week. Until now, I thought that where I was supposed to be was always more important than where I wanted to be. I don't plan to make that mistake any more. Can you help me get home?"

As the pilots urged Shane to re-board the plane, Shane noticed Cade standing at the end of the plane's terminal. Cade nodded his head, and Shane gave a knowing look in reply.

The shift had begun...

Client-Conscious
Prospecting™